Passing It Along:
Wisdom from Corrections Staff

Volume 1

Caterina G. Spinaris, Ph.D.
Editor

Florence, Colorado

Passing It Along: Wisdom from Corrections Staff—Volume 1
Compiled and edited by Caterina G. Spinaris

Mission of Desert Waters Correctional Outreach
"To promote the occupational, personal and
family well-being of the public safety workforce
through the provision of support, resources
and customized data-driven solutions."

Copyright © 2016 held by the contributing authors. All rights
reserved. The reproduction, distribution, or inclusion in other
publication of materials in this book is prohibited without prior written
permission from the authors. No part of this book may be reproduced
by any means, electronic or otherwise, including information storage
and retrieval systems without permission in writing from the authors.

Cover Photograph 2015 © Copyright Ricardo Villa, 2008,
http://www.greatscenicphotos.com/
Cover design and layout by Mary Dilley

Published by Desert Waters Correctional Outreach (DWCO).
Printed in the U.S.A. by Our Daily Bread Ministries,
Grand Rapids, MI

The views and opinions expressed in this book are those of the
authors, and do not necessarily reflect or represent the views and
opinions held by DWCO Board members, staff, and/or volunteers.
DWCO is not responsible for accuracy of statements made
by authors.

ISBN: 978-1-5323-0139-1 (paper)

This publication may be ordered from:
Desert Waters Correctional Outreach
http://desertwaters.com
719-784-4727
DWCO, P.O. Box 355, Florence, CO 81226-0355

TABLE OF CONTENTS

Dedication 4
Acknowledgments.. 5
Endorsements 6
Chapter 1: How It All Began 9
Chapter 2: New Officer on the Block 13
Chapter 3: Presence... 17
Chapter 4: Doing the Right Thing............................. 21
Chapter 5: I Stand Corrected..................................... 23
Chapter 6: Being an Encourager 27
Chapter 7: Swimming in the Cesspool...................... 33
Chapter 8: Two Paths to Correctional Fatigue 45
Chapter 9: Path to Self-care 59
Chapter 10: One Year Smoke Free! 63
Chapter 11: Emergency Preparedness for the Heart . 67
Chapter 12: Cut or Culled from the Herd? 71
Chapter 13: A Solid Partner 77
Chapter 14: Down Time 83
Chapter 15: "What's Better about Me as a Person
    as a Result of Working in Corrections?" 87
Chapter 16: Of What Qualities Are Effective
    Corrections Staff Comprised? 91
Chapter 17: In Closing... 95

DEDICATION

This volume is dedicated to all
corrections professionals "in the trenches"—
whether in facilities or in the community.
You hold the future of the corrections
profession in your hands!

ACKNOWLEDGMENTS

Desert Waters Correctional Outreach would not have been possible and could not have been sustained without my husband Ted Tudor's quiet dedication and diligent work, often in the background. Ted helped co-found the organization, and since its inception, he has volunteered in many capacities. As he likes to say, thanks to Desert Waters, he is "re-tired."

This volume would not have been possible without the contributions by the authors of the articles included here. Thanks to their passion for the profession, they generously offered their writings to Desert Waters, so we could share them in the Correctional Oasis (our monthly educational publication), and in this booklet.

This volume has also benefited greatly from the careful review, suggestions and editing of Gregory Morton, our ever-passionate Training Manager with the burning desire to move the corrections profession forward.

It also benefited from the proofreading of "eagle-eyes" Judy Myers, my sister-in-law and tireless volunteer administrative assistant. Thank you for your relentless attention to detail.

And lastly—but firstly—to my mother, Eleni Spinari, for making so many things possible. She and my deceased father, Christos Spinaris, were the first Desert Waters volunteers that we put to work, stuffing envelopes for the Correctional Oasis mailing (which at the time was done hard copy, by regular mail). My parents' support and encouragement helped sustain me in multiple ways over the years, and still does.

ENDORSEMENTS

Working in the correctional field can be both rewarding and challenging. We don't always realize the effects that being in such an oftentimes negative environment can have on our personality and soul. This booklet provides real life experiences from folks who have walked in your shoes and truly get what you do. I believe the experiences shared here can be of benefit for staff just starting on their correctional journey, and also serve as a reminder for staff who have done their time. Thank you, Desert Waters, for giving the corrections professional a place to feel appreciated and understood!

~ Pamela J Ploughe, Warden (Retired), Colorado Department of Corrections

A great book, full of valuable insights and useful information. A must read for new and experienced correctional professionals alike.

~ Lt. Brent Parker, Fremont County Sheriff's Office; Colorado Department of Corrections (retired)

This volume tells the frank truth about "criminal justice," and I do not mean the "PC" version, but the honest, day to day life of loyal, dedicated, selfless professionals who serve and protect our society. It is poignant, candid, broad-brushed, and directed in a meaningful manner to those interested in entering the field of corrections, as well as those presently serving in corrections. The application of this information from the newbie to the seasoned veteran can help promote healthy public safety for the inmates, personnel, and the society at large.

~ Ron Sands, LMHC, CEAP, Jacksonville Sheriff's Office (retired)

For those who walk the walk and complete the circle of law enforcement that lies deep within the shadows: these articles are written for you. They are written by front line warriors who have shared in our battle, both mentally and physically. And within these articles we find some rarely spoken truth about our profession.

~ Anthony Gangi, host of Tier Talk and CorrectionsOne columnist

Chapter 1

How It All Began

The year was 2005, and Desert Waters Correctional Outreach was two years old. I was contacted by a person in our community who had heard of Desert Waters' mission. She asked if I would consider talking with a friend of hers, a retired corrections professional, who was having a hard time. Following his retirement, he was missing prison work.

Of course I agreed to talk to him, and she gave me his phone number. I called him right away, and that is how I first met Wes Connett, also known to many of you by his pen name—The Old Screw. Two hours into our phone conversation, I was struck by the realization that, thanks to their experience, retired (and active) corrections professionals carry about with them a tremendous and invaluable wealth of information about corrections work. This includes hard-won practical wisdom, do's and don'ts in dealing with offenders and other staff, humor, the history and evolution of correctional practices, and true stories that sound more like fiction. It soon became obvious to me that all that experience should not lay dormant or go to waste. That we must find ways to pass it along to other staff, as words of instruction, words of admonition, and words of encouragement. My vision for this was and remains that each one could and should teach many.

I asked the Old Screw to consider writing articles for the Correctional Oasis, based on what he had learned over his 35 years' security/custody corrections career. To my great joy, he said YES! And that started him on the path of becoming a published author and a blessing to many across the country and around the world.

Over the years, other corrections staff and family members also contributed articles to the Correctional Oasis, sharing their experiences and reflections with others in the profession.

We at Desert Waters believe that the time has now come to produce a selection of these articles in what we hope will be a series of volumes, entitled "Passing It Along: Wisdom from Corrections Staff." This is the first volume, and it offers a sampling of articles that address a variety of topics ranging from professionalism to family matters.

The purpose of this volume, and hopefully subsequent ones to follow, is to present basic principles and tips that contribute to the health of individual corrections professionals and the health of corrections workplace cultures.

We hope and trust that you will find the material to be helpful, at times uplifting and at times sobering. As you know only too well, corrections work can be very challenging. These articles address some of the pertinent issues that impact corrections professionals and their families, and offer some suggestions for ways to have a successful and satisfying career, as well as a good home life.

So, kick back, read, enjoy, reflect, and put relevant tips to practice!

Caterina Spinaris
DWCO Executive Director

Chapter 2

New Officer on the Block
The Old Screw

Being a new Officer in Corrections is something hard to tell anyone about. It stirs up all kinds of emotions:

- Thrill—knowing that not everyone can do our job.

- A little fear—knowing that in our line of work we might not go home someday.

- Doubt—not knowing if we will be able to handle our jobs and meet everyone's requirements.

- Hope—that we will not let our loved ones or fellow Officers down.

Almost every new Officer wonders, "How do I treat the inmates? Do I let them know who is boss? Do I act as if I'm human?"

A few will try to be good ol' boys and act friendly toward the inmates. A few will try to show how big and bad they are. The smart ones will watch the experienced staff. Of course sometimes that doesn't work because veteran staff may have their own problems. In the end it all boils down to a training experience as you learn what to do, what not to do, and why.

So treat every assignment as a learning experience. If you make a mistake, tell someone before the inmates do or before they act as if they are protecting you. Inmates love it when new Officers make mistakes. What they love even more is when you try to cover your mistake up. I guarantee you, whatever you cover up, someday will come back to haunt you. When you make a mistake, it'd be best that you let your supervisor know right away, before inmates start working on you.

New staff looks for approval, but they must not seek it from the inmates. If inmates tell new staff that they like it better when they are on duty, staff need to stop, step back, and review how they are handling things. When you hear this from an inmate, you can be sure of one thing: you are doing something wrong. Not every new Officer will mess up this way, but again not every new Officer will be there at the end of six months or a year. No one expects new staff to do everything correctly right off the bat. But if you are ready to learn, get ready to learn from your mistakes and others'.

If an inmate tells you, "I do this all the time when Officer so-and-so is on duty," tell them you will check it out and see if it is OK. Until then, they must wait for that other officer to come back on duty. The more they protest, the more you know you have made the right decision by not giving in.

New Officers tend to overreact and that is part of the learning curve. If you catch yourself getting uptight, stop, count to ten, take a deep breath, and continue.

Chapter 2: New Officer on the Block

New staff must realize that the inmates will continue to check you out, and will try to push your buttons and manipulate you to see if it will work. If you lose it, they won.

New staff must also learn not to get caught up in the rumor mill. At times Corrections is a very boring job. Judge each staff member by the way they treat you, not by the bad word someone puts out on them. The Officer someone badmouthed may be the same Officer who puts his life on the line for you in a crisis. Yes, that old grouch that people put down may just be tired of all the cowboys and seeing so many staff come and go. If approached with respect, he may be only too happy to help you all he can. I've been there and I've seen it happen.

Take care,
The Old Screw

Wes Connett has been writing for the Correctional Oasis since 2005, using the pen name "The Old Screw." He has worked for over 35 years in corrections, most of them as a Corrections Officer in three States—Missouri, Kansas, and Colorado. He retired as a Lieutenant.

Chapter 3

Presence

Alice Domann

There is no corrections officer big enough to walk into a pod full of inmates and not be outnumbered. The size of an officer is not the determining factor as to whether or not an individual will succeed as a corrections professional. Along the same lines, gender is no more of a determining factor than size is. Many people in fact think that the presence of women staff helps keep the atmosphere of the facility calmer and more at an even keel.

Now, the word "presence" is the key. I define presence as the way you carry yourself—confident, head up, making eye contact, not walking like a victim, professional and taking pride in your appearance. Presence also comes from knowing your job and the rules you are expected to follow and enforce.

Presence for the inmate means they know you will, without exception, enforce your Department's rules, and enforce them fairly and in the same way with all inmates. In other words, if you tell one inmate to tuck his shirt in or wear his ID properly, you tell all inmates to do so when needed, without exception. You do not vary.

You are the one who toes the line. They just follow you.

Inmates will also not respect you if you do not respect yourself. You show self-respect again by your presence, i.e., how you carry yourself and how you enforce the rules. It is a rule that they are not allowed to abuse you or any other staff member. If you allow them to abuse you, they will not respect you. You have to show you command respect by doing just that ... commanding it. Don't let an inmate "front you off" in the presence of other inmates. They lose respect when they are fronted off, and, to their way of thinking, so will you. If an inmate makes an inappropriate comment to you—says you look sexy, calls you a bitch, whatever—take him aside and advise him that you expect to be treated with respect and, if he can't comply with your expectation, you will take disciplinary action.

Sometimes you may not act quickly enough or in the way you would have liked. That's OK. They will make that same mistake again. In corrections you always have time to plan for a future you know is coming. Always write a narrative of the incident and advise the inmate you will be informing your supervisor so that they know that a third party will be involved. Let them know you don't keep secrets.

We have a high concentration of manipulators, predators and others with severe personality disorders in a prison population. I am not smart enough to tell by looking at one of these guys that he's harmless, and neither are you. So don't let an inmate try to be your friend. If they want to be your friend you can safely assume that it is for their good, not yours.

Maintain a professional distance. If you fail to do that,

inmates will lose respect for your authority. We are not here to play their game. They are here to learn ours. Professional distance does not mean that you cannot be pleasant, say "Hello," talk about the weather or the game, or look at pictures of an inmate's family. Professional distance means that you do all these things without divulging any of your own personal information. When you talk about the game, don't say what your brother or son thought about it. When you look at pictures of his family, don't talk about your own.

The only thing an inmate needs to know about you is that you are here to do your job. Remember, you toe the line, so that they will toe the line. We do this work to change their behavioral patterns. We make them follow rules so that they learn to follow rules. We make them respect us, so that they learn to respect others. We draw the line, because they can't or won't. We do not allow them to abuse us in any way, because they are here to learn not to make victims.

You may be surprised to hear that your job is that important. It is. You are here to administer the policies of your Department of Corrections and to fulfill its Mission Statement. That's it.

If the requirements of this job conform to your personal values and life philosophy, you may have picked the right career. If not, you need to keep looking.

Alice Domann is a happily retired 30-year local and state law enforcement professional, who has worked as a corrections officer and as a counselor.

Chapter 4

Doing the Right Thing
Anonymous Jail C.O.

In our line of work, the question often is, do we do what's right or do we say that something is "the right thing to do given the situation?"

In a correctional environment we are charged with carrying out our duties according to the law. Following my department's rules and regulations and policy and procedures (r/r pnp), if I saw a fight between two inmates and knew it stemmed from a problem on the street (that this was a revenge fight), and the person seeking revenge won, what is my responsibility? Under r/r pnp I should lock both down and write them up. Now, I may know that inmate B did a great injustice to inmate A's family, and this was payback. Do I let it slide like nothing happened or not? In jail the right thing is the write-up and lockdown. That's the rule and law.

Another scenario. I catch a staff member who is also a friend passing off contraband—nothing dangerous—to an inmate. A casual mention to the staff member that he/she shouldn't be doing that should suffice, but the situation persists. Do I do the right thing and move on to my supervisor, or is it the right thing to ignore it since it is "blue" and it's not my problem, and the coworker will hang him/herself eventually? The right thing is the first one—tell the supervisor. That's the r/r pnp. If I don't, the plot can thicken in many ways. Security is compromised. Also, what if he/she gets caught, and somehow my name pops up, that I knew about the contraband? Now I just bought into the whole ball of wax with him/her.

Third scenario. An officer gets set up by an inmate. The inmate has been constantly harassed by the officer, and I know it. I can see the C.O. is about to get in some kind of trouble. Do I do the right thing and jump in to help him, or is it the right thing to let him get his "just desserts" since he's a smart aleck anyway, and the inmate deserves to get even? Under r/r pnp, I need to run to my coworker's aid.

The conclusion: **Follow the rules. Don't come up with your own justice.** You may take some guff, but rules are in place to keep us safe. So "doing the right thing" and "it's the right thing to do" hopefully become one and the same.

Chapter 5

I Stand Corrected
Janet Narum

When you get in trouble at work, the words can sting….

- "And why…exactly…did you let that inmate out of his cell? Do you realize that put us all at risk?"
- "She was highly offended. You may have thought it was a casual conversation in the parking lot but she thought you were rude."
- "You threw the evidence away? What reason could you possibly have for doing that?"
- "That was confidential information and you left it sitting by that computer for anybody to see."
- "That email was rude and unprofessional."
- "I asked you as my supervisor not to share that information with my coworkers, but you did it anyway!"
- "I need an explanation as to why you lost your temper in front of coworkers and inmates."
- "Do you realize how much money your mistake cost the Department?"

Ouch! Being corrected is painful. We hate to make mistakes, especially if we are hard-working and dedicated employees. And when it happens, some of us try to cope by taking off on one of the following modes of "transportation."

Blaming-Others-Bus
1. It's not my fault. I watched other people do it the same way.
2. If he hadn't been talking so loud, I would have been able to think under pressure.
3. They're too picky.

Victim-Van
1. It doesn't matter what I do, they always criticize me.
2. I get targeted because they're jealous.

Taunting-Yourself-Train
1. How could I be such an idiot?
2. When will I ever learn?

Holding Ourselves Accountable

Corrections Mission Statements often speak of "holding offenders accountable." But, do we practice accountability with ourselves?

According to Webster's dictionary, accountability means: an obligation or willingness to accept responsibility for one's action. Blaming others, playing the victim, and taunting ourselves are not accepting responsibility nor are they making things right.

Sometimes staff actually role-model after some inmates and shirk accountability. Staff have observed some immature inmates blaming others and fleeing responsibility. Then they find themselves actually taking on the same attitudes and characteristics. They take the immature route rather than the mature one.

Accountability Builds Trust

I frequently cite a text entitled *The Speed of Trust: The One Thing That Changes Everything*. Basically, this book deals with what each one of us can do to increase trust in our personal lives and at work. If you've read it, you've heard about the 13 Behaviors of people who are often trusted by others. One of those behaviors is "Practice Accountability". The authors cited a 2002 Golin/Harris poll where "assuming personal responsibility and accountability" was ranked as the second-highest factor in building trust.

People will trust us more if we take responsibility for our mistakes. As correctional employees, stress can run high because mistakes can put lives at risk. Mistakes also cost time and money. But, the good news is that we have a uniquely human ability to improve our skills, make things right, and get better.

"Yes, I let the inmate out of his cell. That was my mistake and I reported it. I understand this put us at risk and I will not make this kind of mistake again."

"I apologize for talking with your coworkers about those issues that you asked to be kept just between us. There is no excuse and I sincerely apologize for this breach of confidence."

Stand Up. It Takes Guts To Work Here.

Consider this term for a minute: "I stand corrected." Feeling beat up and hiding out doesn't help our mistakes although we may need a bit of time to process what has happened. However, shrugging our shoulders and lowering our eyes for a long period of time won't fix the problem. To stand corrected means to stand tall, muster up courage, admit our mistakes, and make every effort to get better at what we do. Or consider this phrase: "You don't have to take this lying down." As we all know, it takes guts to work here. It takes guts to role-model pro-social behavior by taking responsibility for our mistakes.

As courageous people, we can face mistakes and believe strongly in our own ability to improve. Correctional employees with guts are willing to stand right here and be corrected.

Janet Narum has 20 years of experience working in correctional environments in the states of Washington and Oregon, and recently received her M.S. in Criminal Justice. She presently works for Central Oregon Community College as the Education Director at Deer Ridge Correctional Institution.

Chapter 6

Being an Encourager
Lt. Jason Horn

I remember that when I was little my dad would always tell me how proud he was for something I had done, such as washing the dishes or taking out the trash, without being told to do so. I never really thought much about why dad was giving me praise for completing the chores I was expected to do in the first place. As a matter of fact, I often got tired of hearing it, thinking it was getting old or even downright annoying.

As I think back on it, what dad was doing was rewarding my actions by offering encouragement to me for the most routine of tasks. That encouragement also showed me that my father was aware I was completing my chores, and he appreciated my doing those sometimes mundane tasks. Dad was no fool, he got me to do the things I really didn't care to do by using something as simple as a healthy dose of encouragement.

Let's fast forward about 25 years to today, and expound on this subject of encouragement, and how we can use it in our workplace to get the most monotonous, and seemingly thankless, tasks completed.

So, I want to address the question of why we should encourage one another.

In corrections the whole idea of encouragement often

gets forgotten. We all know that the job of corrections can vary from boring to highly exciting in a matter of seconds. The boring part involves going through the same expected routines over and over again. Because of the repetition, bosses don't take notice, unless something does not get done or gets done wrong. After doing the same thing daily with no thanks, the job can seem unrewarding. Corrections is also a job where sometimes things need to get done immediately in order to make sure everyone concerned stays safe. Going from one thing to another, again it's easy to forget to say thank you or to provide encouragement.

Without some form of encouragement, we begin to think the boss wants a robot, not a living, breathing, human being. We become disgruntled and bitter that we work so hard, yet people who really matter to us, like our bosses, tend not to notice our efforts. This becomes a vicious cycle that begets employees that feel unappreciated and bummed out, and are not motivated to complete their mundane tasks.

I think it is worth visiting what Merriam Webster's dictionary has to say about the word encouragement. According to Webster's, encouragement is:

- the act of making something more appealing or more likely to happen;
- something that makes someone more determined, hopeful, or confident;
- something that makes someone more likely to do something.

Encouragement is much more than someone acting as

Chapter 6: Being an Encourager

your cheering section. It is the act of making someone more determined to do their job, and providing them hope in the process. It also alludes to making someone want to do a better job by encouraging them. All in all, the definition of encouragement is more or less providing someone the motivation to want to do a better job.

So, in saying all of that about encouragement, I would like to provide some ideas about how to start the process of encouraging each other in the workplace:

1. **Be about encouraging others, not about being encouraged.** Depending on how far you would like to go with it, being an encourager can be a way of life. It is easy to sit back and let someone come along and encourage you. I suggest you turn that expectation around and try encouraging others. Pass it along. Despite it being hard at first, as time goes on the act of encouraging others becomes easier, and possibly more rewarding than receiving encouragement.

2. **Encourage from the top down, and from the bottom up.** As far as the top down approach goes, it is only obvious that those who do the grunt work need some much deserved encouragement. We however often overlook the supervisors that seem to have the "cushy" jobs in the air conditioned offices, away from all of the offenders. The reality though is, the upper level management have it rough too, just in different ways. Why not encourage those who have the ability to make a bigger impact for

positive change in our work lives? It is always a good thing to thank your supervisors for whatever positive thing or things they have done for you. We shouldn't wait to encourage certain people, we should be encouraging wherever and whenever possible.

3. **Look for any opportunity to encourage someone.** It is very easy to drone on through your day, and not see anything positive come of it. It is much easier to miss those moments when you could tell someone "thank you," or "great job!" We should always be looking for those moments when a pick-me-up would be appropriate to give a coworker or a supervisor.

4. **Try to see the good in others.** It is impossible to give someone a genuine word of encouragement if all you see in them is the negative. Try to find just one thing that you could comment on about that person. Maybe they did a very good job at calmly speaking to an offender. Or, perhaps this person did a good job at filling out a particular piece of paperwork. Maybe they come to work consistently. The only thing you need to do then is to offer that person some uplifting words.

Work, work, work at it! Rome wasn't built in a day, and doing something that feels foreign will take some time. However, I would venture to say that it will become easier the more you practice, and possibly become so rewarding for you, it becomes like an

Chapter 6: Being an Encourager

addiction in a good way. When you start being a consistent encourager, you will set off a contagious effect that will ripple throughout the workplace.

Encouragement serves us in many ways. It helps pick us up when we are down, and as Mr. Webster said, it increases the likelihood someone will want to do the right thing. It also can make a lasting impression on someone who otherwise would choose to do something drastic to themselves. We are a corrections family, and family takes care of one another. I hardly think we would ever let one of our blood relatives be discouraged if we could do something about it. Families stick together through thick and thin. And we need to do the same with our corrections family.

If we begin to see ourselves as catalysts for something positive, then so, so much more positive will come from it. I encourage you to take these steps today, and see just how much satisfaction you will get out of doing that. After all, your corrections family's morale, and possibly their lives depend on it. Because I believe author Steve Goodier said it best when he said: "Who do you spend time with? Criticizers or encouragers? Surround yourself with those who believe in you. Your life is too important for anything less." So be an encourager that others can be drawn to!

Jason Horn is a Lieutenant at the Missouri Department of Corrections, Farmington Correctional Center. His foundation is rooted in the Gospel of Jesus Christ.

Chapter 7

Swimming in the Cesspool
Sgt. Chad Leivan

It all starts so easy. Just a few moments of discompassion. Nothing major, just a few seconds of irrational thoughts coupled with the ability to separate the reality of what you are facing from the few random thoughts of meanness. It doesn't happen all at once. You don't disassociate from society in one quick move. You slowly slip into an area that most will never go to and can never go to and come back from. You don't think about what is going on, but rather you think about how to handle it with the most tact and get through it with your sanity. A few jokes with others in the field, the ability to think about how death or pain can make it worse or better. But the ability to think about it in those terms leads you down the road, and discompassion for others is where you end up.

You can stop it, you can make it go away and start to feel for others. That is what separates the bad from the good. **The sad thing is that so many of the good are starting to not stop it. You stay there longer and longer after each incident and you have a harder and harder time leaving the realm of this evil streak that seems to always be looming under the surface.** You see the world in terms of what you like to do and how things are messed up and what you could do to help, but it isn't always a positive change you think about to make it better.

That's when you develop your own personal, internal cesspool of mind and heart, as you swim in the external cesspool at your corrections workplace.

Once in the internal cesspool, it is hard to get out. When you swim in the external "cess" daily for work, it gets harder and harder to get the stink off. When you work every day to make ends meet, and getting into the external cesspool is how you do that, at some point you become acclimated. It is like jumping into a cold pond. It is only cold when you first jump in. You soon don't notice it and just keep swimming, and getting out is colder than being in.

Handling it can be accomplished, but not through most conventional ways. You can't just walk away and hope it gets better. You must start handling it from the beginning. Just like the cold pond. Getting out gets easier if you already have a dry warm towel to get into, and you must learn what that can be and prepare to bring it with you.

You have got to start by knowing that only through positive social interactions will you be able to get out of your personal cesspool. You must start with having positive coping skills, by being active, physically and mentally, and by not taking work home. You must not let the internal cesspool build up in you.

Most of the time the internal "cess" starts with fear. The jobs you do in the external cesspool are generally dangerous and can be life-threatening and at first the front of disconcern comes up to displace the real feelings of fear. You soon learn to control your fear and adrenaline, and become accustomed to turning them on and off.

Some never conquer their fear and they become addicted to it. Those are not good team members. In a short order they can become a liability and risk to everyone around them. Others learn to shut off their fear and adrenaline and never react accordingly to them. They also become a problem and liability.

The best ones though learn to use fear to their benefit. Fear has a place. Not all the time, but when necessary it brings a side of caution. The increased speed and strength during adrenaline dumps can make a situation better and much smoother, and being able to control both is a start in getting yourself under control. It isn't an easy task, but it can be accomplished.

The feelings that arise during or after an incident cause some to conclude that they are not able to handle the cesspool. That isn't a bad thing. In some ways the ones that try and see that they are not able to stay are just as strong or stronger than the ones that stay in the cesspool. Most don't make it long, but those that do usually have long-term mental conflicts from what they have done and seen.

Sometimes emotion is a liability in these situations. It isn't that having emotions is wrong, but the ability to become cold and calculating leads to the desired result in some situations. But losing the ability to feel compassion and humaneness is a very big reality for those who spend too much time without their emotions or with them being a liability. And without compassion and humaneness, the internal cesspool grows.

The way to maintain healthy emotions is by learning when and where to have them and display them, which is not the easiest of tasks. You must understand the nature of human interaction, and learn to read people. Some will never develop the skills of reading people, some will never be able to turn on or shut off emotions. Neither of these issues is necessarily a negative. It just proves that some can do this job well and some can't.

There always will be some individuals in the external "cess." So you have to have those willing to risk life, limb and mental stability to be in the pool with them. Those that work too long in the "cess" are more than likely going to exhibit some sort of long-term effect and this should be addressed.

Addressing the issues well is not done with self-medication. A lot of long-term professional cesspool swimmers are home self-medicators. Whether it is prescription drugs or alcohol, this self-medication is not positive. Working too long in the pool also leads to high blood pressure, obesity, heart problems, lung problems, exposure to diseases at a higher rate than normal and much, much more.

To address these issues, start with acknowledging them. Most professionals will brush all but death. They will never admit something bothers them. They may admit they are out of the shape they used to be in, but they don't motivate each other to get back in shape, and most don't diligently seek a workout regimen that will facilitate a healthy body. The work schedule kept is part of the problem. Little sleep, inappropriate diet and constant on-call status keep most off a normal schedule. Unlike some jobs, the cesspool is open 24 hours a day and 7 days a week. It doesn't take holidays or weekends off. In fact, it is usually busier on those days and the days leading up to them. It makes having a normal schedule hard. Things are done when they can be, and some are put off to the last minute or not done at all.

Admitting weakness is a strength in and of itself. It proves that not all things can be fixed by bottling them up when it comes to health. It also suggests that maybe by dealing with the problems out loud they can get better.

Working daily where you will be verbally, and possibly, physically abused and threatened, and your family threatened, and then doing it all over again tomorrow, takes an individual with strong self-control and a strong motivation. Some take these threats and this abuse personally. Those that do generally don't last long in the pool. Some blow them off and forget them. They too deal with them less than effectively. Most of the threats are just verbal manipulation toward desired ends, but there are a few that may be real and need to be taken seriously and at face value.

The best way to deal with the verbal abuse every day is to treat it like what it is. Words. Verbal abuse is something that divorces can be based on, lawsuits are won on, but they are just part of the job in the pool.

Every day the professionals that jump into the cesspool for the sake of the rest of society get verbally abused more in one shift than most will have in their entire life. Taking personally what someone else says about how you look, who you are, what you wear, what you think, is something that must be avoided. If you were really exactly as they described you, you wouldn't be willing to do what you do for others and work where loss of limb and life are always a possibility.

The games played with verbal abuse and threats are a bully type of game. Those who live in the cesspool think that if they can make you feel inferior you will listen to them. The true professional will not come back with the same type of language toward them, but will remain calm and professional while speaking with them. That can be one of the hardest hurdles to overcome, but it must be overcome. Berating or insulting someone who has just insulted you is what you would expect from children on the playground, not from professionals.

Threats are a different thing all together. Threats need not be tolerated, and need not be followed by threats in return. They should be documented in reports for future reference. Threats of all nature pose a dangerous game of "will they or will they not attempt, at some time, to follow through." By documenting them you allow yourself the protection of having formal documentation that would justify defense of your person or family if the situation were to ever arise. By the same token part of the stress of living in the external cesspool as a professional is learning to be vigilant but not paranoid. That is a fine line. It is completely

Chapter 7: Swimming in the Cesspool

unrealistic to believe either extreme: that you are ready at all times, or that threats are always just a game. So the stress of protecting yourself at work and knowing that you must protect your family when away from work is a huge psychological distraction and burden of long-term employment, and unnecessary stress when you are off work.

The external cesspool is always looking for another full-time occupant, someone willing to sell out their morality for a quick profit or more powerful position in the pool, and the guardians are just as susceptible as the people who are either stuck there or choose to be there. **You must constantly be on guard for the ones wanting to permanently suck you into the cesspool as a participant and not the guardian.**

Most guardians know their limitations and are willing to ask for help (usually when they are hugely outside their limits), but it isn't the big steps outside your limitations that get you caught in the internal pool. **The small voids that separate you from your humaneness and morality are what make most of the professionals change for the worse.** By reading people and seeing that some will never be more than pool junkies, you desensitize yourself and your actions to those who make no effort to get themselves out—and that is where the problems start.

Seeing good can be easy, but seeing the potential for good is not so easy. **When you start to give in to the dehumanization of others, you are morally corrupting yourself and begin to get the mean streak you can't shut off.** There are times when being mean works, but for the most part, mean is just that—mean. It has very little benefit other than immediate satisfaction for the one being mean, and it only hardens the one you are being mean to.

What makes working in the external pool worth it is the ability to see the potential for good and to offer guidance to bring someone out of the pool by showing them a side of a person they may not see daily. All people are human and are deserving of decent behavior until they pose a significant threat to you. They deserve decent treatment and the avoidance of bullying at all costs.

That doesn't mean that pressuring someone to tell the truth is bullying. It means that getting there should not be done with invalid threats or lies. It also means that finding the human side in most people will get you further and help your mental stability more than bullying. Bullying is something that naturally comes from too much time in the "cess." You start using bullying tactics that you see around you, and then they become a lifestyle. You blend work with your social life and begin to bully others outside work. The ability to force your will on others in your social life is easier when you get your way or force your will on others on the job. Or when you don't have any way to force your will on others on the job, you do that outside the job. Either way it results in bullying for personal gain, which is the reason for so many divorces or unhappy marriages of those that work in the "cess."

The ones who daily risk their lives to protect those in the pool are true heroes, but as with all hard chargers,

Chapter 7: Swimming in the Cesspool

there is a side effect of long-term interaction in those environments. Changes take place in those who work daily on the edge or in the "cess." The families of those in the field are the ones that truly take the brunt of the issues, and the alpha male/female attitude of the "cess" professionals causes them to shy away from help. Most of the changes that gradually come on are seen and dealt with amongst family and friends, but their advice is disregarded by the person receiving the advice. It is the family that can offer the most help, but may be the last source of help sought out and received.

Therefore, there needs to be a way to account for and take care of the mental and physical well-being of those in that type of work. Those willing to risk their lives for others deserve enough respect to at least have the proper systems in place to make sure that work is work and home is home. There are options, none free, some cheaper than others, but they all will require activity from policy makers and others in the field to be introduced and accepted.

The first thing that would help is physical fitness tests and retests to maintain a bare minimum of physical fitness for the job. There also needs to be included a full physical assessment that would determine the total physical health and potentially increase the service life and longevity as a whole for the person working in the "cess." This should not be looked at as something that is dreaded by the worker, but as something in which they can show improvement and achievement. These tests should not be pre-scheduled, but random. At least annually, but not the same time every year. Surprise means that the worker must maintain a minimum level of fitness at all times to be able to pass and also means they are more prepared to handle the physical stressors of the job all the time.

Psychological monitoring needs to start with pre-employment and be followed up at least annually to monitor the mental health and well-being of the worker. Small changes in attitude should be noted by supervisors and noted in the personnel file for the psychological monitors so that they can see the changes over time. These items need to be confidential and not placed in the personnel file for review by others, unless the changes are unsafe for the worker or fellow workers or may lead to legal implications, at which time they need to be seen and addressed by the highest ranking person and reporting persons only. This area must be approached with caution as to not turn into a harassment situation. The psychological monitors need to set up a system that evaluates the safety and ability to reason as well as check for irrational behavior when things get out of hand. Including high stress items in the test and checking for how the worker functions/responds can predict the outcome of situations that may occur in the "cess". The test also needs to be embraced by the higher ranking workers and taken very seriously. Most will see this kind of testing as intrusive and a witch hunt, but it is not that, and should not be addressed as that. It should be addressed as a way to help maintain the social ability of the worker to maintain a life of health and normalcy. The test should also include input from the family of the worker and any changes in home life noted.

The psychological professional should be available at

all times for the worker to address personal or work-related problems to help maintain mental health for the long-term. The psychological professional should be embraced and looked at as a resource to help deal with the stress at work and home, and balancing working in the "cess" and living without paranoia, anger issues, control issues or any other long-term debilitating mental problems. And chaplains could also be available to help maintain internal health of professional cesspool swimmers.

To handle the issues as described here will take forward thinking and proactive leadership that should not look at the cost as prohibitive, but as an investment in the long-term continuing service of much needed experienced "cess" swimmers. The better adjusted the swimmer is in the different areas they swim in—"cess" and regular life—the longer and better service that can be expected and enjoyed by all.

We have not spoken about the financial assistance or benefit packages that should be attached to such jobs. Those topics are for another day. The issues above are addressed from the standpoint of someone who has dealt with these issues and worked in the cesspool for five years.

I have fought and still fight daily with control issues, anger issues, discompassion, dehumanization, physical fitness, family problems and more. I have witnessed addiction issues and other problems and still see all of them daily with my fellow swimmers. I know first-hand what happens when issues are ignored by leadership and the morale decrease of having to daily work with mentally unstable coworkers.

Having said all of that, the one thing that makes it all worthwhile is the one good day when you help someone who is truly grateful for the help they receive when for months nobody has been grateful.

You don't swim in the "cess" because you like the smell. You swim in the "cess" because someone always needs to be pulled out or saved on their worst day, and you are there to do it.

Don't ever give up. Stay strong and keep a life preserver handy for those that need it—yourself included, and you can work in the "cess" for years and still come out smelling like a rose.

Sgt. Chad Leivan has worked in corrections for 10 years, including 5 years in a maximum security Administrative Segregation as a COI. He currently works for the Missouri Department of Public Safety as a Military Security Officer

Chapter 8

Two Paths to Corrections Fatigue
By Gregory Morton

Dr. Caterina Spinaris has defined Corrections Fatigue as the cumulative negative transformation of a corrections staff's personality, health and functioning, and of the workplace culture, as a result of attempts to adapt to the demands of the corrections environment.

Having worked in corrections for thirty plus years, my opinion is that this is a common condition. It occurs as a result of ongoing contact with varied and frequent corrections workplace stressors. It can be gradual, hardly noticeable, yet continuous, occurring non-stop, much like a constant erosion. And sometimes it is fed by major incidents, causing an internal landslide.

The effects of Corrections Fatigue are generally negative, from a reduction in either emotional and/or physical health to relationship challenges and increased substance use. Attendance issues, turnover, morale, the motivation to perform well and to contribute as a team member can also be affected.

Steps for reducing those negative effects can start with recognition of the events that lead to Corrections Fatigue. At the extreme ends of the workforce continuum there are two paths that can take staff to that place. I believe that no one is totally immune, no matter where we start.

A Sometimes Polarized Workforce

People find value in corrections work for many reasons. Some staff find value in contributing to public safety by ensuring that institutionalized offenders are kept away from our streets and homes, and by controlling and disciplining the behavior of those offenders. After all, they, by their own actions, have demonstrated that they can't control and discipline their own behavior, whether incarcerated or in the community. Field service agents may find value in their work by controlling and disciplining the behavior of those on their caseload in the community. Whether in facilities or in the community, these employees have more of a cop's way of thinking.

Other staff find value in contributing to public safety by taking an extremely raw, untutored or addicted human being and helping him or her learn new, pro-social ways of living in society. These have more of a counselor's way of thinking.

On a good day, most staff fulfil some of the tasks of both of these roles, recognizing the balance needed between the two—custody/security and rehabilitation. In doing so they honor those whose personal style or assigned role differs from their own. On a bad day staff may get out of balance and go too far on one end of the spectrum (cop or counselor), and over-react and blame others at the opposite end for complicating work life.

Granted, these polarized stereotypes are over-generalizations. In well-run facilities, offices and organizations these extreme opposites are reduced, if not eliminated. However, they do represent two common employee profiles. As a result, they may provide insights into different ways that Corrections Fatigue occurs.

In an effort to bring some humor to a very serious topic, we will hereby christen each group according to their stereotyped characteristics—cop Harry Callahan/sharpshooter Annie Oakley on one hand, and kind Mother Teresa/humanitarian Albert Schweitzer on the other. As we work through the Corrections Fatigue model, we will recognize these over-generalizations for what they are, but also use them for what they might teach us about our vulnerabilities.

Corrections Fatigue And Harry Callahan/Annie Oakley—Introduction

The mindset goes like this: "Where discipline does not exist, it must be applied. If ignored, it must be enforced. That's why I took this job. I'm disciplined, I'm reliable, and I'm thorough. Things don't get past me. I believe in standards and will do my part every day to ensure that either they are met or accountability is assigned. We all want to go home at the end of the day. In correctional environments this doesn't happen by itself. Safety requires attention to detail, rules of conduct, enforcement of those rules, and compliance with the enforcement."

Corrections Fatigue And Mother Teresa/Albert Schweitzer—Introduction

A man was walking on a beach. A heavy tide had washed hundreds of starfish onto the sand. The man was picking up starfish one at a time and throwing them back in the water. Another man said, "Hey buddy, what are you doing? There are too many of them. You won't be able to help them all." The first man kept walking and picking up starfish, throwing them one at a time back in the water. "I helped that one," he said.

You believe that if you're not part of the solution, you're part of the problem. And so you take a job in corrections and tell people, "If I only help just one, it will all be worth it." Your friends answer back, "The world needs more people like you. If you can't do it, nobody can. You're a bigger person than I am."

Corrections Fatigue And Harry Callahan/Annie Oakley—What Happens Next

"Where discipline does not exist, it must be applied. That's why I took this job. Things don't get past me. I believe in standards and will do my part to ensure that either they are met or accountability is assigned. Community, staff and even offender safety is job number one. We all want to go home at the end of the day. In correctional environments this doesn't happen by itself. It requires attention to detail, rules of conduct, enforcement of those rules and compliance with the enforcement. Good security is not convenient. Good security starts with attentive staff."

A lot of offenders don't play by the rules. They lie, steal, manipulate, and assault others. They may want to hurt you personally, or if not you, your partner. And if not your partner, then whoever happens to be walking by.

Chapter 8: Two Paths to Corrections Fatigue

When we drive up to our local ATM, in the safety of our locked vehicle, we may get lazy and not pay attention to our surroundings. But when we are in an unfamiliar community, in a bad part of town, at night, by ourselves, and we have to walk outside to an ATM as much as we don't want to, we are constantly vigilant and on guard. There may or may not be danger in the immediate area, but since we don't know for sure we recognize the potential and act as if there is. In correctional environments, every work day is like that for us.

Except for when it's worse and the danger isn't just potential, but real. I help break up a fight between gang members. I find drugs or weapons in a residence by myself surrounded by the offender and his family. I confront theft in the act. I discover sexual abuse. I come upon an individual hanging or bleeding profusely. I have to react instantly, no matter what I was doing or thinking about just a few seconds earlier. And my reaction needs to include giving orders to bystanders, reaching for my radio and/or handcuffs, keeping myself safe, knowing that there will be a written report at the end of all this so I need to pay attention to everything, and watch for whatever other event this might just be a diversion for. Constant vigilance is a requirement, a life-saving adaptation. Without it, the system falls apart and may take us with it. That's why standards are important in the first place. Watch for violations. Never look the other way. Confront as necessary. Take care of the details and the big things will take care of themselves. Get the work done, make sure offenders comply. Have a safe day. Go home.

Since simple requests may not get followed, we start

giving orders. Since orders can be misheard or ignored, we start raising our voice. Since loud orders frequently provoke a loud response we add some emotion for emphasis. Since emotion provokes emotion we have our comeback ready. Since comebacks can seem like an invitation to an argument, we carry a handy toolbox of threats which we use as required. We can easily get all caught up in this, get all upset and fuming, escalating situations trying to control and get compliance.

But you know what? The offender didn't really have anything else going on that day anyway. Messing with you is just good entertainment. And if he is slick enough, you can't even do a behavior report since he was, "Just askin', so what're you getting all worked up about?"

So you walk away frustrated, ready for the next idiot to come along. Or you write him up anyway. Well, it's not like he's never been dinged before and if it doesn't happen today with you, then it'll probably happen soon enough with somebody else. Ain't no big thing to him.

But it is a big thing to you. And maybe it ends up being an even bigger thing to your loved ones.

Because what do these interactions cost us? When does over-vigilance at work become a permanent lifestyle? When do those exciting workplace incidents become trauma that can be triggered off the job? When do standards and accountability and compliance go from a workplace responsibility to a family rule that only you seem to know about? When do our simple family requests that get ignored because the TV's too loud or somebody else had a tough day too, become orders? When does that "next idiot to come along" turn out to be a family member?

All you were trying to do was do a good job, keep yourself and others safe, follow the rules, hold offenders accountable and here you are now, aware of every social violation that happens around you, hostile in your interactions, aggressive when others aren't, distant from your family, triggered by strangers, just generally pissed off everywhere you go.

Corrections Fatigue is the cumulative negative transformation of one's self or personality, health and functioning, and of the workplace culture, as a result of unsatisfactory attempts to adapt to the demands of the corrections workplace.

For you, cop Harry Callahan and sharpshooter Annie Oakley, your very work ethic, composed of the pro-social characteristics of dependability, accountability and vigilance, taken to the extreme, has conspired to put you on edge every moment of your day, every day of your life, regardless of where you are and who you are with.

Corrections Fatigue And Mother Teresa/Albert Schweitzer—What Happens Next

If you're not part of the solution, you're part of the problem. And so you take a job in corrections and tell people, "If I only help just one, it will all be worth it." Your friends answer back, "The world needs more people like you. If you can't do it, nobody can. You're a bigger person than I am." Compassion is your passion. You say, "I know that change is up to them, but if they've never had a real chance, what can you expect?" And, "In order to be successful, you have to know what success even looks like first. Everyone can change."

And that's what's so maddening. Because while you know that everyone can change, offenders you work with act as if that's not true at all. If they just believed it as strongly as you did, they wouldn't live in a cage every day. There wouldn't be a trail of victims behind them. They would tell the truth, have a happy life. Instead, they act as if they don't care. So you work harder, put more effort into that famous compassion of yours. If you want it more, you'll convince them and they'll want it too. You just wish they worked harder too, so you didn't feel like you were the only one paddling the canoe.

Then the first offender you sweated over and really connected with violates and gets locked up again. And then the second one. They both have reasons, although when you dig down into the logic and facts, the reasons sound more like excuses. And you feel like you've been conned.

Then the minor cases of being taken advantage of, which you absorbed as the price of doing business with this population – the back talk, the sloppy work, the nuisance contraband – culminate in a major policy violation by you, which gets you noticed by the administration in all the wrong ways. And still you have to go back to your same job because by now you

Chapter 8: Two Paths to Corrections Fatigue

have economic pressures that complicate your philosophical belief system. Now you have to face a failure you never saw coming. You worry that one incident will become a reputation. The negative behaviors you've put up with don't slacken out of consideration for the situation you're now in. If anything, they seem to have increased.

And then a few more get re-incarcerated. The excuses become transparent and repetitious. The negative feedback you get from your job doesn't stop. When someone points out that corrections people almost never see their successes, since successful released offenders simply become citizens and vanish from the system, you perk up slightly. You remember what your friends said when you started, "The world needs more people like you. If you can't do it, nobody can." You get more training which results in some added motivation, so you come back stronger than ever.

Until you get conned again. And then somebody steals your stapler, and someone else makes you the butt of a joke. And you have to do somebody else's work because they called in. And the copy machine always runs out of paper when you absolutely need it. Your reputation follows you everywhere you go. When a new crop of idealistic employees cycles through, the ones you like shake their heads and leave, the ones you don't like stay. Manipulation and excuses are so common, you get good at them yourself. Your family complains, but you don't care since work takes all the caring you can muster.

Negative event after negative event becomes like

those infamous straws on that camel's back. Your compassion passion now strikes you as a personal vulnerability that somebody should have warned you about. You're angry that you haven't achieved what you originally set out to do. The world is not a better place. Yeah, you helped a few. But the few get swallowed up by the overwhelming many. Maybe helping just one is not really enough success to build a whole career on. The next time an idealistic employee cycle starts again, you just scoff. Welcome to the city dump. Did you bring your shovel to clean the streets after the parade has gone by? Always lock your stapler up and if you're going to use the copy machine, make sure you keep a ream of paper stashed in a secret place. If you don't do it, nobody's gonna do it for you.

Corrections Fatigue is the cumulative negative transformation of one's self or personality, health and functioning, and of the workplace culture, as a result of unsatisfactory attempts to adapt to the demands of the corrections workplace.

For you, kind Mother Teresa and humanitarian Albert Schweitzer, the ideals that brought you to this calling become a pathway that leads to being taken advantage of over and over again, with the result that those beliefs have soured to such a degree that they are now a burden that has worn deeply into your soul regardless of where you are and who you are with.

Regardless of our personal path, Corrections Fatigue originates in a need for coping with, surviving in and adapting to an abnormal human environment, and as a

Chapter 8: Two Paths to Corrections Fatigue

result, it can be called a normal and natural occurrence. It is normal because it becomes the norm—it happens to virtually all corrections employees merely because of the stressful and dangerous workplace we choose for our employment and because of our need for self-preservation within that workplace. It is natural because it is to be expected and can even be predicted.

Unfortunately, while normal and natural for the corrections worker, the cognitive/emotional/physical effects of Corrections Fatigue are generally negative. The consequences are all too familiar.

In an effort to bring some humor to a very serious topic, we christened two extreme tendencies according to their stereotypical characteristics – Harry Callahan/Annie Oakley on one hand, Mother Teresa/Albert Schweitzer on the other. Not every employee turns into the two stereotypes we have caricatured. Most of us are slighter versions of the two extremes, or we switch from one aspect to the other as the need arises. Many of us have some element of both since our work causes us to play two roles simultaneously. On a good day, most staff fulfill some of the tasks of both of these roles, recognizing the balance needed between the two—custody/security and rehabilitation. In doing so they honor those whose personal style or assigned role differs from their own. On a bad day staff may get out of balance and go too far on one end of the spectrum (cop or counselor), and over-react and blame others at the opposite end for complicating work life.

As you look back on Harry and Annie, valuable corrections professionals that they are, where would you have intervened with them? What would you have said to Teresa and Albert? How would you have helped these peers see what they were experiencing and the toll it was taking?

At this point in the development of the profession, correctional employees are the people who understand best the draining emotional burden under which coworkers often labor. Yes, professional therapists provide valuable, life-changing, even life-saving work. They should be called upon more frequently than they currently are. And actually, that might be one of the pieces of advice you give a coworker: See a counselor, call the Employee Assistance Program, work with a professional.

But you're there, in it together, shift after shift. So as you consider yourself and your coworkers, what could you do tomorrow, or tonight even, when you go back to work in your environment? How can you lend a hand? What service can you provide to your coworkers?

Consider these two ideas.

Validation: Validating another person's experience has the effect of stabilizing the cognitive/emotional ground upon which he or she is standing. When we find out that someone understands our issues, we're likely to think, "Well, at least I'm not crazy." That's validation, the recognition that the difficulty we're facing is real, that it truly deserves our attention and should be problem-solved. This recognition of the issues is normalizing and confirming. It allows the person to take two steps back from the problem, to

Chapter 8: Two Paths to Corrections Fatigue

clear their emotional air, to reframe the consequences, to find one's strengths, to gather resources, and take on future events with focus and energy.

(Note: While it's important to validate a colleague's perspective at work, it's equally important not to take sides in an interpersonal disagreement. Validating one coworker while diminishing another does not improve the organization. Remember, we don't just suffer from Corrections Fatigue. In some cases, we cause it.)

Support: You're there. You see things, you hear things. You know the profession. You know who's having a hard time. We talk about First Responders a lot in corrections. You can be an informal First Responder to the onset of Corrections Fatigue at any time, once you're attuned to it. A supportive, caring listener could be the key to someone's healthy adaptation to the environment rather than the opposite. Some jurisdictions recruit and train peer supporters to be designated First Responders, though even they are more frequently used for traumatic events than for the daily wear and tear.

This should not replace working with a professional therapist for issues that are too complex for a layperson, but the immediacy of caring support can keep incidents from festering within a person. In addition, a tradition of positive, health affirming, on-duty support for the challenges of the profession would change the work environment for the better in general.

Ask yourself: After an interaction with me, are

colleagues closer to finding solutions for their issues or are they one more step down the road toward Corrections Fatigue?

Greg Morton started his Corrections career in 1975 at the Oregon State Penitentiary and then worked in Staff Training, primarily at the department level, for three decades. He retired in 2010 after returning to the same Penitentiary building where he began, doing offender treatment work. He became affiliated with Desert Waters Correctional Outreach at that time and currently serves as DWCO's Training Manager.

Chapter 9

Path to Self-care
Alice Domann

I have been asked how I have managed to maintain all these years in a male institution with such apparent ease. My answer is that I was old enough when I started out to know who I was and nobody was going to shake that. **Know who you are, know how you want to be known, know what you want and how you are going to get it.** Maybe that's the start of a path for the pursuit of self-care.

We rarely initiate anything in corrections without a planned form of action. Why should our lives not get the same considered reflection? Whether we make the right choices or the wrong choices, we are responsible for those choices. So, what ARE the most important things in your life? Kids? Relationships? School? Sports? Music? Work? Choose what these are for you. List them in order of importance to you and how much time you plan on devoting to them each week. What will be your strategies to deal with interruptions like changes in work schedule, working overtime, bringing a rough day home with you? With many of us, work is NOT anywhere near the most important part of our lives, so don't let it overshadow the life you really want to build. Corrections is very intense. It can take over your life if you are not vigilant. The comradeship you feel at work is great, but, that's part-time life. You want to build a whole, full-time life.

Do what you can to leave work at work. Put a picture of your kids, bike, spouse, whatever is important to you, in the car and look at it to visually remove your brain from where it has been, so that by the time you get home you are ready to make the switchover. Find something that works for you. You hear about problems corrections people deal with at home. I sometimes wonder if that is because we take the work adrenaline with us and invite chaotic behavior in our personal lives. If we want to change people's reactions to us, we need to change our actions toward them. Once you are at home, you are not on a response team, you are not expected to react to violations of 44-12-10 or whatever else. You're HOME! That's the good place. Relax and enjoy those around you. It's OK.

Consider, choose and plan what you want. Write the plan out, refer to it daily and you will be less likely to lose track of what is important to you. Let those around you in on what you are doing and ask for help when you need it.

You also have to make decisions about relationships at work. We have married couples at work and others in relationships. It seems to work for those who can leave romance at home and not bring it to work. I decided a long time ago that my personal life and work life were separate. I've seen too many complications from failed or inappropriate relationships and, in a prison, that puts you in a weakened position as far as both staff and inmates are concerned. The job is hard enough without that complication. When you meet the employee who can't respect your decision, stand your ground. They will flit off to some-

Chapter 9: Path to Self-care

one else soon enough. And you can thank God you missed that sorry boat. The women and men who are Corrections Professionals will appreciate your steadfastness and reliability.

There's more to the path. Since corrections can be so consuming, let's make sure we control it before it controls us. Why did you get into corrections? Did you get into it as a longtime interest or did you need a job and benefits to make a living for your family, or both? Where does it fit into your life plans? Do you plan on advancing in rank or to another section of corrections? If so, what is your timeline? How do you plan to accomplish this? Do you want to advance in seniority just enough so you can pick the shift that is most advantageous for your family? Who do you see as a mentor? Will they accept you as someone to teach? What do you need to learn? Have you decided you don't intend to stay in corrections? What else do you want to do? How will you accomplish your new goal?

So consider, choose and make a plan. Nobody can or should tell you how your life is to be lived. That's your job. If you do it, it will express self-love, you will pay proper attention to the important things in your life, and everyone in it will get a much better YOU.

Chapter 10

One Year Smoke Free!
Anonymous Corrections Educator

One year ago today I smoked my last cigarette. I have not inhaled so much as one puff in that time. I decided way ahead of time to quit, picked a date and used Chantix for a few weeks to help me along at first. I chose my birthday as my first cigarette-free day as a gift to myself. As with any addiction, one must choose to leave it because they are tired of it, see negative effects and are willing to change. I couldn't do it for my husband and children, my financial gain, my social status or to ease my guilt. If those things were enough to cause an addict to quit, there would be no such thing as an addict.

You see, this decision was made because I was tired of making myself sick. I was tired of being driven by a drug and letting it dictate my every thought and action. I knew if I didn't quit I would one day die from it, and I want to live. I decided to take control of my life and quit because I knew that I'd be better for it in so many ways. In exchange for me taking care of myself, all of the other benefits of not smoking fell into place as well. I saw a quote the other day that said something like, "I thought when I fixed my life, it would fix my drinking. Little did I know the opposite was true." Perfectly stated.

Addiction is a very powerful and evil beast. I am not smoke-free because I'm strong. I am smoke-free because I made a decision to surrender and then reach out for help from God, my family/friends, an online support network and my doctor. I didn't do any of this alone nor could I have. It has been a very difficult and long road. I decide each day I wake up not to smoke and hope that tomorrow I'm able to do the same.

Smoking is like all other addictions. I don't care if it's cigarettes, gambling, eating, heroin, alcohol, etc. Addiction is addiction is addiction. The only way to ever overcome it for me was: be ready and do it for you, no one else; surrender, and then reach out for help; take one day at a time, and one step at a time, to continue growing, strengthening and becoming the healthiest version of yourself you can be by using the tools you learn along the way.

This year has been a journey to find myself and an understanding of so much more than me all at once. My dad, who was also a correctional officer, was an addict. He took his own life because he felt unable to find inner peace and happiness. I'm not sure why he used or why he was constantly at battle with himself. I'm not sure he knew. He tried unsuccessfully to quit many times for all the wrong reasons. He always quit for what he stood to lose, never for what he stood to gain.

I have chosen to learn to do what he felt he could not. By watching him endure his own addiction, pain, and ultimate death, I have learned to be free. I started this journey this year for me. I continue it knowing he would be proud. I'm no stronger or wiser than he was.

Chapter 10: One Year Smoke Free!

I've actively chosen to learn and grow from the final lesson he left for me. He paid the ultimate price for that lesson and I refuse to let it be for nothing. I choose to use it to help me be all that I can be for myself and those around me.

I still have a long way to go and each day I will continue to try. Today I am free and have an inner peace and happiness that I feel so blessed to have received. God is good and has guided me on this journey. He gives me all that I need to be successful, and I don't doubt for one minute that he will continue to do just that.

Now, onto my cake addiction............

The author of this article is a female correctional professional that has worked for over 17 years in the adult male prison system in various positions, including that of a correctional officer.

66

Chapter 11

Emergency Preparedness for the Heart
Anonymous Corrections Educator

Remember the day you got the call from the prison? You were hired! You felt such extreme relief and excitement! Your young wife shrieked with delight when you got off the phone. "Let's take the kids to Chuck E. Cheese's and celebrate."

Over dinner, you made your plans. Life was going to improve with two incomes again. Heck, you could do Disneyland, the beach, maybe even a cruise.

Your six-year old daughter, with wide eyes, asked questions about prisons, prisoners, and handcuffs.

When your heads hit your pillows that night, you softly conversed about the costs of college for the kids, planning for retirement, and just before falling asleep, you even considered a little brother for your son.

You knew what you wanted that day: You wanted a career to support your family.

It's now five years later. You've done so well. You smile when you think about how much the prison appreciates you. You never called in sick. You would work any shift at any time. You were willing to promote. And…you made friends at work. In fact, Administration loves you. Hard-working people like you. And a smart, beautiful, dedicated woman loves you. She understands what you do. You never tire of what you can talk about. She "gets" you in a way that your wife could never understand.

And now you know what you want today: You want a woman who supports your career, because you have replaced your family with your career.

This happens way too often. We become enthusiastic about a career, and lose enthusiasm for the ones we love the most. Work becomes our home and as that happens, we dread going home because home now has become hard work.

One way to preserve your family is to plan ahead, like you do for emergencies at work. You have the ability—and responsibility—to prepare for what could threaten your home life, long before it is threatened. **Plan ahead!**

So here are some thoughts for *Emergency Preparedness for Your Heart.*

1. No matter what shift I work, I will express my love to my loved ones at home at least once every 24 hours.
2. At work, I will not have any conversations with coworkers that I would not want my spouse to overhear.
3. I will be loyal to my spouse in my thoughts and conversations. I will not fantasize about a coworker.

Chapter 11: Emergency Preparedness for the Heart 69

4. If I find myself attracted to a coworker, I will recognize this as an emergency.
    A. I will absolutely seek professional counseling as soon as possible.
    B. I will carefully guard my conversations and thoughts. I will never seek out that individual to have conversations, other than what is absolutely necessary for my work.
    C. I will never say to this person, "If I wasn't married, I would be interested in you." This is nearly always the first conversation that leads to an affair.
    D. I will talk warmly about my spouse and home life with coworkers if possible.
    E. I will make every effort to not travel alone with a coworker whom I find to be attractive. If I am required to do so, I will ask for someone else to go along. If that is not possible, I will set up an accountability system, such as frequent phone calls home and/or to a trusted friend or spiritual advisor who knows the situation and who has agreed to help me navigate through this experience safely.
    F. If I need to be out of town for work, I will only go out in groups and I will be in my room early and I will call my spouse. I will never be alone with a coworker whom I find to be attractive.
5. If I feel lonely at work, I will think of my loved ones at home. I will not try and find loved ones at work.

Chapter 12

Boundary Violations: Cut or Culled from The Herd?

Susan Jones, Ph.D.

Most correctional employees can recall hearing about incidents where employees are "walked out" of the facility after a relationship with an inmate is uncovered. Sometimes these episodes catch us by surprise, and sometimes we remark that we knew that was going to happen eventually. Many of us have even been close enough to the incidents or investigation to see the fallout upon not only the employee involved in the incident, but upon many others. The fallout can include the end of a marriage, financial ruin, and even criminal prosecution.

This story is not unique to one agency or to one type of facility. I have yet to talk to a correctional professional, from any agency, that can't relate similar events. So why does this happen?

As I pondered this issue, I was reminded of a term I knew from my childhood on the farm. I compared this process of boundary violations to that of being cut from the herd. Yet I couldn't understand how in this instance, an outside predator (an inmate) could move in, identify a weakness, and remove this staff member from our team. How could this happen over and over again on our watch? I wondered about this for years, as I watched these events happen time and time again.

As a correctional professional, I was determined to learn more about this process, so that the numbers of boundary violations could be reduced. As I promoted through the ranks to the level of warden, I was involved in many discussions that revolved around this issue. I listened to many colleagues at different levels of the system who were dumbfounded with the numbers of incidents. The same question surfaced over and over: "How can this keep happening?"

I started looking for answers in the research literature, and I quickly realized that very little research has been done in this area. What we do know usually comes from statistical reports from agencies or from inmates involved in relationships with staff. The piece that was missing was the description of the process from the involved staff member's point of view.

From an administrator's point of view, this absence of information from the involved employee was easily understood: we never ask them. However, even if we did ask, the employee probably wouldn't tell us because they would run the risk of increased administrative or criminal sanctions. So, in the absence of information, we have done what all good bureaucracies have done: we fill in the gaps of knowledge ourselves. In other words, we make it up.

I am not speaking in the abstract here, but from specific experiences where the tale of how an inmate "cut" an employee from our herd (team) was expanded from one day to the next. For instance, someone would see the former employee in the community or they would talk to the inmate who had been involved, and tidbits

Chapter 12: Boundary Violations

of information from those exchanges would be added to the story. These stories then took their place in the agency's history and were passed on as facts.

When I began to seriously look for answers regarding boundary violations, I realized that without the information from the staff involved, we were destined to make no progress towards a true understanding. As a result, I chose to examine this issue from the point of view of the women involved. My Ph.D. dissertation, entitled *A Portrait of Boundary Violations*, is a record of that research, but it is a starting point of this research, not an ending. Even though I have completed the dissertation, I have continued to seek out opportunities to hear the "facts" from the point of view of women who have left corrections after becoming involved in relationships with inmates.

The women who have trusted me with their stories have been involved in relationships that cross a minor boundary all the way to those who have crossed a criminal or sexual boundary. I am continually amazed with the courage of these women to share with me very private and complicated stories. For some, I see an appreciation that someone is finally asking them. For others, it is a hope that by sharing this information they can help someone else; perhaps prevent someone else from making the same choices they have made.

Not all the stories that I have had the privilege of receiving point to a singular cause or process, but there is one theme that I find in many of these stories.

Most of these employees were not cut from the herd,

but instead, **they were culled from the herd**.

To be culled from a herd means that the herd removes or rejects a member. If you are talking about animals, this may mean that the member of the herd is abandoned and left to survive on their own in an environment where resources are scarce and where support is absent. I believe that the same explanation applies to people, to correctional employees, who have been rejected by their team. These employees have often found themselves wandering around, in a dangerous environment, without the support or the resources afforded as part of a team. It should really not come as a surprise when they find support from inmates.

This explanation is difficult to accept because it goes against a corrections culture that says "we are a team; we are there for each other—WE ARE FAMILY." But it is this same culture that often harshly judges and rejects those who don't fit in. Sometimes these are people that have a different background, or those who traveled an unusual career path that led them to corrections work. Sometimes these rejected team members violated a fundamental cultural expectation, such as "ratting" on a fellow staff member. Sometimes these rejected staff members did something far less heinous, like they approached a problem with an inmate in a nontraditional manner and eliminated the need for force.

At any rate, the possibility exists that we must consider the fact that some of our coworkers who have moved away from our team to become involved with inmates do so after we "culled" them from our herd.

Looking at this issue in this way is uncomfortable, and even as a corrections retiree I am haunted by the actions that I may have taken or failed to take that allowed some members of our team to feel rejected.

I write this as a point for contemplation for us all. Could there be some merit to this idea that, in some cases at least, employees sought relationships with inmates AFTER they were excluded from professional relationships and interactions as part of the correctional team?

Dr. Susan Jones retired from the Colorado corrections after 31 years. She worked in community corrections as well as the adult correctional system. She is now devoting her time and energy to research related to correctional employees and their work environment.

Chapter 13

A Solid Partner
Phil Haskett

The summer day was bright, crisp and cloudless. Although the Parade Ground looked so small, I stood there with pride as my wife of 10 years watched on with our two small children as I was presented with the Dux of Course award on the final day of training at the South Australian Academy for Corrections. No thought entered my mind about how strenuous it was going to be for my family over the next 20 years wondering if I was going to come home safe and well; if I was going to ignore them because I had a crappy day; if I was going to retreat into a bottle of beer for the night feeling sorry for myself at having a prisoner win one over me; or if I was going to snap at every remark my wife or kids made because the daily exposure of working "behind the wire" made me more and more act like an inmate.

No. This was one of the best days of my life. I was the best. I was top of the class of 1990!!

Now, 20 years later, I sit here in early retirement because of PTSD due to an incident that happened 12 years ago, ashamed of myself for being a harsh partner and father. For being self-centered. For being secretive about my worries and not confiding in them for support. For keeping them at arm's length and keeping them out of my inner world.

I feel no sense of pride for coming home in a bad mood, sometimes injured, often tired, occasionally feeling unappreciated for doing a solid day's work, angry because a roster was changed by a Supervisor who favoured a "mate" to a softer post, scared and distant towards them after being treated as a perpetrator and not as a justice administrator. Sometimes I felt like I had done something wrong, when in fact all I did was go to work, putting in my 12 hours at 100% (and some).

On days like these I'd go home expecting a champagne reception each time. Did I ever ask about their worries? No. I was too set in a self-centered mentality. Me first, second and always.

But now I have just completed 20 years working in a negative industry that gave me no skills whatsoever to cope with the emotional strain I was to put my family through. I have other skills, other knowledge, but none to make me a better person outside the wire, or to my family. I now have to be "re-programmed." Thankfully, I have found the means.

Not once did I ask my family what they thought of my chosen career. Not once did I listen when my wife said, "Don't talk to us like one of your prisoners" or "Do you know how badly you speak to us lately?" or "Why won't you listen to us?"

Through this, I am still married to a great wife, who gave me two fantastic boys and who has stood by me through thick and thin. This is what I call a solid partner. Yes, we have had our disagreements (let's not pull punches. . . they were loud verbal fights) and hours of a strained atmosphere in the house. But 29 years of marriage has beaten 20 years of Corrections.

I am an Australian-born British Army veteran who served in the finest regiment in the British Army, the Coldstream Guards; who was once a leader of fighting men in action; a respected non-commissioned officer; a Queen's Guard who shone on duty at the palaces for the tourists to photograph; someone who always looked after his men and always sided with the underdog; the one who always came out of battle smiling, ready to go do it again the next day and the next and the next, whenever asked. Never complaining; never questioning. But today I feel beaten. Not by an adversary in physical battle or in a battle of wits, but beaten by a system that needs new direction and one which needs to listen to more people like "The Old Screw" instead of "bean counters." In the end, staff are a more valuable asset than the financial "bottom line."

And yet, although feeling beaten in some aspects, I feel a sense of achievement for what I have gained in the past, both in the military and in corrections. Attaining the positions of leadership. Making hard decisions that have saved subordinates from injury. Making myself available for anyone who wanted a shoulder to cry on. Starting initiatives that have forged the birth of an organization that helps correctional staff in times of crisis. The awards and letters of recognition for bravery, courage and dedication are nice to reflect on, but really are hollow compared to a colleague who just says, "Thank you for just being you, mate."

But as much as I cherish those thoughts, I feel that I am responsible for letting my family down. It was my choice to enter the world of corrections, not theirs. It was my choice to let myself be dragged down to a lower level of caring when I should have separated work from home. I just was never shown that there was an alternative choice to make apart from the one I took in those 20 years.

This first week in retirement has not given me a sense of joy at what lies ahead. Instead, it is giving me joy to know that I am responding to help from others. Help to learn how to leave the negatives behind. Help to think more positively. Help to leave my poor attitude behind. Help to leave the withdrawal from my family behind. Help to regain the unquestionable love and devotion I once had for my family.

Now I have to learn how to treat my wife and family like I should have done long ago. Now is not too late to ask for forgiveness and for me to give back to them what I had so many times demanded from them. The one thing above all ... unconditional love and respect. Now in retirement I have some "firsts" to achieve.

- My first goal: "To revert to the past person who my wife married and who my kids first called Dad."
- My first lesson to learn: "The glass is now always half full, not half empty."
- My first observation to make: "It doesn't matter how tough you think you are; **it is not a sign of weakness to ask for help!**"

Chapter 13: A Solid Partner

- My first promise to make: "To realize that there are always people far worse off than I thought I ever was."
- My first hope to wish for: "That I be forgiven for my past failures and be remembered for trying my best."

And remember: **You are stronger by accepting help than by denying you need help.**

Chapter 14

Down Time

The Old Screw

There are two words in corrections that are very critical but not understood by most families and even new Staff—DOWN TIME.

The need for down time can be the cause of a lot of misunderstanding and arguments among Officers and their spouses. The spouses usually have difficulty grasping why the Officers need space when they get home from work, why they need to read a book, watch TV, exercise, or work on something instead of talking with their partners. The need for down time can also cause a lot of hurt and anger from children who do not comprehend why daddy or mommy wants to be left alone for a little while after getting home from work.

Some staff will argue that they can leave work and step right into family life—that they feel no stress from their work, that "there's nothing to it." Only God knows how many times this was said before the divorce. (I know. I am on my second marriage.) Anytime we put our life on the line day after day, no matter what type of facility we work in, the thought that someday we may not come home is always in the back of our minds. We fear (here's the forbidden word!) that someday that lovely wife or husband or small children might not see us again.

Male Officers have a real problem with their emotions. They think it makes them less of a man to admit to experiencing stress, and so they try to hide these feelings. In my opinion it takes a braver man to admit to the stress.

The truth is that in our line of work the adrenaline starts pumping sometimes even before we get to work. Just thinking about what happened there the day before, or what we have to deal with once we get there, can get us going. And the adrenaline surge doesn't stop just because we're heading home at the end of our shift. It continues to circulate in our system when we walk in the door.

That's why we need the down time. We need the time and space to shift from the stress-filled work world to family life.

Some staff think that a few beers or other drinks after work with fellow Officers are the way to relax, and that they even deserve that kind of break. Many an affair started during this kind of "choir practice."

Affairs also happen because an Officer thinks that only another Officer will understand them. Officers can come to believe this when their spouses don't accept and respect their need for down time.

It seems at times like getting a divorce is a requirement for the job. Many of the problems may start with the unmet need for down time.

For those of you married to an Officer, it is rough

Chapter 14: Down Time

when your spouse comes home from work and doesn't want to talk or do anything with you for a while. You may think, "What did I do wrong?" The answer usually is, "Nothing." It's just that **your spouse needs DOWN TIME!** Officers don't like to bring their work home. Some of the things that happen in our profession are very crude or downright sick. By not talking about them, they think they are protecting you. Even when both spouses work in corrections it is sometimes hard to relate. Yes, even these families need down time.

The best solution is when the spouses are open and explain things to each other. This can be hard to do, but the reward is a more stable marriage and better understanding of one another.

So, when your spouse who works in corrections seems to be withdrawn and quiet, give them breathing space. Take the kids and go for a ride, or do something that your spouse can join in on later, when he or she is ready.

I am not a counselor or psychologist, but I will try to explain corrections to any family member who wants to ask. To me, we are all brothers and sisters, and I will try to help in any way I can. I neither know all the answers nor claim to, but I come from over three decades of working in corrections and know very well the need for down time.

I am proud of the fine men and women that I have worked with over the years. No matter what anyone says about corrections, be proud of who you are and what you do. Not everyone will walk among killers and rapists—and sometimes worse—**with only a pen** to help control the people milling around them.

Take care,
The Old Screw

Chapter 15

"What's Better about Me as a Person as a Result of Working in Corrections?"
Gregory Morton

Desert Waters' course entitled From Corrections Fatigue to Fulfillment™ covers a great deal of territory. It allows staff to explore the challenges inherent to the corrections profession; it validates the difficult times that staff may have experienced on and off the job trying to handle those challenges; it gives groups the time and opportunity to ask themselves "What are WE going to do about it?"; and it even connects our work life to our home life.

And then, late in the afternoon, it asks the question found in the title of this chapter: "What's better about me as a person as a result of working in corrections?" Answers vary of course. That's the beauty of it. But my favorite answer has come to be, "I've never thought to ask myself that question." So let's spend a few minutes and do just exactly that.

What's better about you as a person as a result of having worked in Corrections?

Are you more dependable and reliable? "Yes," people say. "I understand the consequences of not following through or not being available when somebody needs me, because of all the times it's happened to me." Or, "Doing something so that people don't trust me anymore? I can't live with that."

Are you grateful for the good things you have in life? "Oh boy, absolutely," people say. "Having my freedom limited would be terrible." "I don't take my freedom for granted anymore."

And how about being able to respond to problems other people want to ignore? Or being able to talk to difficult people that everyone else in your family is afraid of? A lot of those answers end up being real stories, "The neighbor's dog got hit by a car and broke its leg. They just lost it and didn't know what to do." Or, "There was this time at a family picnic…."

Are you more honest, more accountable? A lot of people say "Yes" to that. "I would much rather have someone like my boss hear from me first what I did than from someone else. Hiding something only makes it worse. Even when it's hard. Especially when it's hard." Or, "Not facing up to the mistakes I've made is a slippery slope. Once someone gets comfortable doing that, they can cause all kinds of damage to others and not care."

But what is most amazing about the answers people give, regardless of what they are, is the shift in tone in the room that comes with the answers. The room becomes filled with a sense of pride and integrity, an unshakeable confidence, a reality that is both genuine and very, very strong. Most people don't have to do what we do. Most people don't have to adapt and overcome like we do. Most people don't have to face the very worst in life and handle it with fortitude and courage. And then come back the next day to do it all over again. And again.

So why don't we ask ourselves that question more frequently? We're really good at asking the opposite – why this work has caused us to gain weight, or to be grouchy, or to get divorced, or call in sick when we're not, or to drink too much, or only sit with our backs to the wall in public, or to not even go out in public anymore, and so on. Ask Corrections employees what they don't like about the job or their agency or their facility or office, and get ready for a 60-minute monologue about every rock they've ever had in their shoe. Frankly, that question is easy to answer. In fact, too easy.

I've come to believe that answering "What's better about me as a person as a result of working in Corrections?" is the fundamental, threshold question on the path to Corrections Fulfillment. That is, it is the required first step on the path. Until we ask ourselves this question, until we each individually conduct the necessary personal assessment to determine what really is better about ourselves as a result of our career choice, we are doomed to be stuck in the cycle of Corrections Fatigue. The question ***"How am I a better person?" is the doorway out.***

The greater, more academic, and also more dramatic concept here is known as Posttraumatic Growth (PTG). As a culture we've started to spend a lot of time focusing on Posttraumatic Stress Disorder (PTSD). And rightfully so. It is a devastating condition if not responded to. But PTG is as valid a psychological concept as PTSD is, and it may well have functionally opposite, neurobiological effects.

PTG is a universal phenomenon and has been well established throughout human history. The arts, specifically literature, drama and, more recently, cinema, are crowded with stories of people transforming themselves as a result of the barriers they have had to overcome. We are entertained by those stories every day. And yet, we rarely apply them to ourselves and our chosen career. We may have experienced real, direct trauma at work. It happens. We all know that. Or we may have experienced indirect trauma through reading, viewing, or just hearing and talking about traumatic events. In either case, trauma has been a part of our professional lives. And while it may have influenced us negatively, as we are oh, so eager to tell people, our ability to overcome it has influenced us positively as well.

So, as you continue on your path to Corrections Fulfillment, it is good to frequently stop and ask yourself, "What's better about me as a person as a result of having worked in Corrections? How have I grown? How have I been transformed? What is stronger about me, smarter, tougher, more resilient?"

And once you have those answers, pass them along.

Chapter 16

Of What Qualities Are Effective Corrections Staff Comprised?

Joe Bouchard

Have you ever thought about what it takes to have success in corrections? Certainly, favorable circumstances are necessary. Yet, even with optimal events, the corrections professional cannot perform as well without positive core traits. What are some core qualities?

A student in my Criminal Justice class was also taking an English class. One of his writing projects was to describe how to do something well. He chose "How to be a great corrections officer" and needed six sources. He asked me to be one of these sources.

I agreed to an interview on one condition. I asked that he consider modifying the topic slightly. I asked that he change it from how to be a great corrections officer to how to become a great corrections staff person. As a programs professional, I cannot speak with authority on custody staff. He agreed and I gave what I deemed are necessary qualities in order to succeed in corrections.

Right off the bat, I said:
1. Ability to follow instructions. After all, in a paramilitary setting, one has to act along the lines of policy and procedure. The chain of command facilitates this.

2. Good sense of humor. The ability to laugh, especially at oneself, is a healthy way to cope with the negativity of the vocation. For a long career, it is better if one has a good sense of humor than a bitter outlook that will always lead to cynicism and disillusionment.

That was enough for the student's project. He needed no more from me. Still, there are many more qualities of which effective corrections staff are comprised. With the two above, I have added eight to round out ten qualities.

3. Broad perspective. Staff need to look at the larger operations in addition to their own area. All areas are important. But the interconnectivity of these areas needs to be conceptualized and brought together through professionalism.

4. Integrity. The person with integrity does what has been promised. There is a dependability that comes with this position. The person who demonstrates integrity does not promise the stars to placate the persistent offender. He promises what he can and stands by his word.

5. Vigilance. This is the ever watchful person. She does not get lost in the boredom and monotony of simple watching. Rather, she watches and reports.

6. Tenacity. Quite simply, someone with this quality does not give up when things become difficult.

7. Objectivity. According to dictionary.com, a person

who is able to remain objective is someone who is not influenced by personal feelings, interpretations, or prejudice; but who acts based on facts. In our quasi-judicial function as corrections staff, we should never be driven by personal feelings. When an offender who you witness committing an offense has proven obnoxious in the past, their old behavior should not be part of the current offense.

8. Flexibility. Although corrections operations are run on predictability, it is wise to be able to think out of the box when necessary. Flexible thinking in situations that require discretion is helpful. This flexibility may provide solutions for vexing operations problems later.

9. Calm command. If you are not in charge, someone else is. Those who possess calm command show those who they lead that everything is under control and that leadership is not an ego trip.

10. "What if?" mindset. This quality is best used when the staff blends in well and looks disinterested and non-threatening. The key is that the person is ready to spring into action as necessary. That is because while watching, the staff person engages in hypotheticals. This is like a shortstop who thinks, "What if the ball is hit here? Where do I throw it?" Then, when the ball is in the neighborhood of the shortstop, it is executed as planned.

Perhaps your list of top qualities for effective corrections staff differs from mine. In the end, it is the interplay of several admirable qualities that make the individual. And then, at the next level, the interplay of good corrections staff is a crucial part of a well-run, safe facility.

Joe Bouchard has been employed with the Michigan Department of Corrections as a Librarian since 1993. These are his opinions and views, and not necessarily those of the Michigan Department of Corrections. His employer is not in any way responsible for the content or accuracy of this material.

Chapter 17

In Closing

This brings us to the end of this volume. For new staff, I hope that reading it has given you some useful tips and ideas, things to look out for or things to put in place in your life to make for a good career in corrections and for a good home life. For veteran staff, this book may have stirred up memories, brought some aspects of your own experience back to mind, reminded you of some basics, or challenged you in some ways. To all our readers we'd like to say, take what fits of what you read—what makes sense to you at this time in your career—and leave the rest. And perhaps revisit this book at a later time. Perhaps something else will get your attention and make sense then.

We welcome your feedback. Please take a few minutes to let us know your thoughts. And/or you may feel inspired to write your own article and send it to us to consider for publication in the Correctional Oasis. You can do both by contacting me through desertwaters.com, by going to About, http://desertwaters.com/?page_id=3674.

Let us continue to make it possible for each one to teach many by sharing your hard-earned wisdom gained through your correctional experience!

Caterina Spinaris

Découvrez aussi chez Milady Romance :

27 NOVEMBRE 2015

- **Emmy Curtis**, Alpha Ops, *Sous l'uniforme*

CE MOIS-CI

- **Catherine Kalengula**, *Keep Calm & Love Me*

27 NOVEMBRE 2015

- **Ruthie Knox**, Roman Holiday, *Un brin de folie*

CE MOIS-CI

- **L.A. Witt**, Tucker Springs, *Soumets-nous à la tentation*

27 NOVEMBRE 2015

- **Tere Michaels**, *Nouveau départ*

Achevé d'imprimer en septembre 2015
Par CPI Brodard & Taupin - La Flèche (France)
N° d'impression : 3013102
Dépôt légal : octobre 2015
Imprimé en France
81121600-1